T. Adeola

STRAIGHT
OUTTA
CONTEXT

Why Google is No Substitute for College in
The Information Age of
#FakeNews & Misinformation.

For information regarding special discounts
for bulk purchases, please contact at

ThinkBeyoundBuzzwords.tech/Bulk-Deal

ISBN-13: 978-1-7364574-0-5

FREE Resource website at

ThinkBeyondBuzzwords.tech/Resources

Cover design by

Michelle A. Bassett

Edited by

Rae Ober

Table of Contents

Acknowledgements

The author would like to express his sincere gratitude to the following:

To the mothers of my children, Tiffany and Michelle. Fatherhood is a sacred thing. I cherish it and our beautiful children. I appreciate you both more than I can express.

To my Obi Wan Kenobi, Uncle Iroh and beloved big brother Hotep, MBA. Thank you for welcoming me into the Hustle University family with open arms.

To Darius Hicks, Aaron Watkins, Branden Morris, MBA and Joey Womack. To say you brothers refined my pitching skills would be an understatement bordering on criminally remiss.

To Liberty White for trusting me to co-host her top-notch production, #BreakfastAndConvos. Working with you is a privilege I don't take for granted.

To my Early Risers cohort facilitators KeAnna Daniels and Gail Francis Johnson. You two had

4

a monster of a task and handled it with grace. Thank you for pouring into all of us.

To Brandy Foster of the ONEIL Center and Wright State University. You're just the best!!

To Audrey Ingram and John Owen of Launch Dayton. Thanks so much for the vibrant community you've created and unwavering support.

To James Oliver Jr., in addition to being one of my favorite guests, the way you pour value into the Black community is a level of awesome I aspire to.

To my We Tha Incubator cohort facilitators and We Tha Plug co-founders Luis Martinez and Christiana Russel. I love y'all - nothing more to say.

Last but never least, Kemo A'akhutera. In many ways this all started with you. In the midst of my trauma, you thought it not robbery to gift me with a FREE ticket to StartUp Grind Global in San Francisco. That one act of kindness has manifested in ways I couldn't imagine and really has been the gift that kept on giving. It's an honor to be a part of your journey and know that I count myself blessed to have you as a part of mine. Let's get it.

Intro: Darth Vee

Gary Vaynerchuk is a Sith Lord! I hate to be the one to tell you that, but it's true. Don't believe me? In *Star Wars Episode III: Revenge of the Sith*, while confronting the newly minted Darth Vader, Obi-Wan Kenobi says, "Only a Sith deals in absolutes". Gary Vee deals almost exclusively in absolutes! As one of the, if not the loudest voices in the un-College movement, Darth Vee cannot be ignored – his many crimes cannot go unpunished. And like a heavy-hearted Obi-Wan, "I will do what I must".

Unlike 99.99% of the actors in this space, I actually have a degree in Digital Marketing. A vocal minority of folks take issue with this off of principle. You got your Gary Vee's and a few other prominent Digital Marketers who don't believe in learning Digital Marketing, or any other skill set, in a University setting. But just stick with me, by the end of this short book I'll expose the erroneous parts to that train of thought as someone who has actually gone through that very process; therefore, I can speak from lived experience instead of opinions and theories.

I should also note that this is my second degree in Digital Marketing. The first was from the school of hard knocks! I tried just Googling it – it didn't go well. So unlike Gary Vee who can only provide you with one side of the coin, you'll get both from me.

Why this book?

A friend of mine is a man by the name of James Oliver Jr. He's a serial entrepreneur and founder of The ParentPreneur Foundation, among many others. Through his foundation I was able to attend Seth Godin's virtual Marketing Seminar. If you don't know who Seth Godin is, a quick Google search will reveal he's kind of a big deal in the Digital Marketing industry.

One of the many lessons that Seth teaches is that Marketers make change happen. That's what we do – we're change agents. I believe this down to my core. I also believe that in the wrong hands, Marketing is the ultimate weapon of mass destruction! That's why it's essential we create more ethical marketers to clean up the industry and root out the bad actors that have left the world upside down.

In the last three months of the 2016 U.S. Presidential election, fake news outperformed real news on Facebook. Don't worry; this is a book about College & Career Readiness, not politics, but what I'm trying to pull out with that example is that most people struggle to identify, categorize and contextualize valid information online – what I call Digital Discernment.

This reality is in stark contrast to the un-College movement that favors finding information online, oftentimes for free, instead of paying for higher education. That tactic can work, assuming you can actually parse out the real from the fake, but unfortunately, most people can't! The ability to identify, categorize and contextualize valid digital information, what I call Digital Discernment is a skill, which means that it can be learned.

When I first started this journey back in 2003/2004, I was very naive. I was a true believer in the Digital Marketing Myth: I can just hop online, make money and I'm good! I don't have to endure people deleting my job application because of my God-given name. The Internet changes everything, right? I'll just blaze my own trail online. How hard can it be? (How very cute I used to be).

I got a quick education on the brutal realities of digital business operations and became disenchanted, but I still love this industry. I love everything about it, warts and all. While I'm a huge fan of Gary Vee (believe it or not), he's one of the main perpetrators of The Digital Marketing Myth. He tends to speak in absolutes that are often oversimplified and void of context. Given the current state of the world young people will inherit, being able to glean the appropriate context is more important than ever.

But really, I'm talking to my younger self. If I knew then what I know now, right? I'm still young, but I'm fresh out of twenties, and on the back half of my thirties as of this writing. I officially have a misspent youth. I'm doing my best to try to rectify that and pass on any nuggets that I've gained over the years. If you're ready, let's go!

Stumbled in Digital Marketing

I started this journey way back in 2003/2004. Back then I was actively trying to avoid corporate life. I didn't want a long commute just to be forced around people I really didn't like. More importantly, I was trying to get away from name discrimination.

Quick story: One day at Sinclair College they had a job fair. An HR Manager from the Beavercreek, OH Lowe's Home Improvement was there. I was studying Civil Construction and Real Estate Investment at the time. I interviewed for a position in the Lumber and Building Materials department and knocked it out the park! She said that if I wanted to work at the Beavercreek Lowe's she could offer me a position on the spot. However, I declined and said I wanted to work at the Dayton Mall Lowe's because it was in walking distance from my apartment. The Beavercreek HR said that she would refer me enthusiastically to the Dayton Mall HR Manager, but that she didn't have the authority to make hiring decisions for another store.

I followed up that next day with the Dayton Mall HR Manager and… nothing! It was like my stellar interview with the Beavercreek HR Manager never happened. But I continue to follow up every two to three weeks because I had been told by the other HR manager that I was shoe in. Nevertheless, the hiring process stalled out and I didn't understand why.

It wasn't until the Dayton Mall HR manager got fired and the HR Coordinator was the acting HR Manager that I finally got hired. She had seen me show up and follow up consistently for months and hired me on the

10

spot. Months later, she shared with me the HR manager was the type that if she could not pronounce your name, she did not call you back – PERIOD! It didn't matter what your resume said or what your qualifications were. If your name was anything other than Jim, Bob or Tom, you were out of luck with her! That, among other reasons, got her fired.

So that's what drove me online in the first place. Forget waiting on racist HR Managers to get fired before I can get a job. I'll just go online and make money! But being as green as a blade of grass, I ran headlong into Network Marketing, MLM, whatever you want to call it. I eventually found my way to Warrior Forum and got into Info-marketing, funnels and all that good stuff. I bottomed out on all of it! I hit rock bottom and was doing penny clicks. You have officially bottomed out when you're doing penny clicks. But that's actually where I saw a banner ad for Full Sail University, which is how I wound up in the degree program.

I tell this story because in my case, I didn't intentionally set out with a career in Digital Marketing in mind. It was more so I knew what I didn't want, and in the process of moving away from those things I backed into Digital Marketing. However, had I been more intentional at the outset I would have gone further faster. I don't want you to make the same mistake! That's why I'm writing this book for you.

Also, I'm an older millennial. I was born in 84'. So, while yes, I'm a "digital native" and grew up with technology, I still remember the 80's. I was only five, but I was there! I remember how things were before – before smartphones and gaming and all of this other stuff. I have a very unique point of view because oftentimes the people who talk at younger generations, not necessarily to us, can't relate.

You are in very capable hands. I'm eminently qualified to speak on the subject of Digital Marketing, specifically the impact of using Google searches on one's career trajectory, at length. Again, I hacked away at it for a decade before getting serious and getting a degree in it. I have a very unique point of view that precious few people can lay claim to. And that's what I'm giving you in this book.

Marketing Disenchanted

What follows is my disenchanted definition of marketing. You're not going to find this in any textbook because it's not widely adopted, but it's as true a definition as you're going to get. Marketing is <u>mass behavior modification that produces a consistent business outcome</u>. We're going to take that point by point.

First one, mass, what do I mean by that? It means you use a form of mass communication. So, it's one-to-many. You're using the Internet, social media, podcasts, etc. If you want to go old school, television, radio & newspaper; but the form of communication that you're using is one-to-many. So, you're using mass media.

Secondly, behavior modification; this is where it gets tricky. You've got to be real careful when you say behavior modification, because people freak out. They go all "big brother" on you and start wearing tinfoil hats because they're worried about mind control and all that nonsense. But the reason I say behavior modification is because like Kings, consumers aren't born – they're made! Nobody comes out of the womb thinking that a sugary bottle of candy is synonymous with happiness, Christmas and polar bears. That didn't just happen on its own. Rather, it was very intentional on the part of Coca-Cola and they spend $Billions every year reinforcing their brand position every year, and to great effect.

This study has been done time and time again. Researchers do a double-blind taste test and 50% of people like the flavor of Pepsi and 50% of people like the flavor of Coke. It's split right down the middle. But if you ask them which they prefer, 70% of people say Coke. Now the 20% that said Coke but chose Pepsi, they're not lying. They weren't being intentionally dishonest, but that's the power of Coke's brand. When done properly, the behavior modification we call branding will override what you can scientifically prove to people.

But it gets much deeper than double-blind taste tests my friend. This case study that I'm about to share, I learned in the degree program and I will never forget this for as long as I live: This guy goes into a Target in Minneapolis, MN and demands to speak with the store manager. He then proceeds to go off on this poor store manager. He's like, "My daughter is only 15 years old and you guys are sending her coupons for baby stuff. Are you trying to encourage her daughter to get pregnant?"

The store manager of course apologizes and is like, "Hey, that stuff comes from corporate. We don't really deal with it here on the store level. But I'll make sure you're taken off the list. I'm really sorry for the mix up, blah,

blah, blah." The next day the guy comes back, and he apologizes to the store manager. He explains, "I guess there were some things going on in my household I wasn't fully aware of. My daughter is due in a couple of months."

Target figured out that this man's daughter was pregnant before he did! They looked at her shopping history and were able to deduce that based on her purchases, not only was she pregnant, but she was in her third trimester of pregnancy. You know those Target and Kroger plus cards they give you in exchange for discounts? The reason you're a "valued customer" and they give you discounts is because they track everything that you buy and use that data to negotiate with their vendors and suppliers.

Now that's freaky in and of itself, but that's not where the whole behavior modification thing comes in. The reason this information is important to retailers is because market studies have shown that people really don't pay attention to advertising. We're creatures of habit. We buy what we buy because that's our brand and that's what we buy; **EXCEPT** during major life moments! Such as having a baby, getting married or divorced, having somebody graduate from College or a kid moving out the house now you're an empty nester, etc.

Shopping behaviors change in very interesting ways. For example, when you get married the type of cereal and toothpaste you buy tends to change. And when you get a divorce the brand of beer that you buy tends to change... really interesting stuff. So as an advertiser, if you can catch people during these major life moments you stand to have a consumer for a number of years. Because again, once that buying behavior gets locked in it doesn't change until the next major life moment comes around.

But because advertisers don't know when these major life events will occur, currently it's necessary to blanket people with offers so as not to miss them when they do roll around. So that's what I mean by behavior modification. No mind control or "Big Brother", just good old fashion advertising with a sprinkle of Big Data.

Last but not least, produces a consistent business. That's what we were just talking about. Any fool can make a sale once or twice, but successful brands want you to come back again and again. That's where success comes in because you can get people to purchase from you repeatedly, that's your cash flow.

So, there you have it; mass behavior modification that produces a consistent business outcome, that's my definition of marketing. Again, you're not going to hear that from anybody else. But from my over a decade of experience, as well as going through a degree program, I'm telling you that's what marketing is. That's what it's about.

Chapter 1: No Tinfoil Hats Allowed

First things first, this book is not, repeat **NOT** about bashing Google. While they're certainly not angels as a company, on the whole the world is a better place for having Google in it. Their stated mission, *"To organize the world's information and make it universally accessible and useful"* is a noble one. But the pursuit of this lofty ideal has birthed more than a few unintended consequences; not least of which are the primary focuses of this book: #FakeNews/Misinformation and the un-College Movement.

Fun fact: I'm birthday twins with the rapper Ice Cube from NWA. In the movie *Straight Outta Compton* based on the game changing rap group Ice Cube is a founding member of, there's a scene where the late Eazy-E gets called out for the graphic nature of the group's lyrics. His response was classic:

"The coke comes from Columbia. – The guns come from Germany. – We ain't got passports."

What I take from that quote, is that a third party set the stage for the crack epidemic that ravaged mostly Black communities in the 1980's; a gruesome and cruel reality reflected in the group's lyrics. It's disingenuous to criticize gangster rap without also criticizing the conditions that created it, specifically the Nixon and Reagan administrations that let the drugs and guns in the country in the first place.

I make a similar claim in this book. Just as it's disingenuous to harshly criticize gangster rap but find no fault with the Nixon and Reagan administrations; it's also disingenuous to blast Facebook for the social blight that is #FakeNews and misinformation but find no fault with Google who created the conditions for the malignancy of #FakeNews and Misinformation to metastasize into full blown social cancer.

Google was never intended as a substitute for College and cannot replace the collegiate experience. As is always the case, the road to this circle of hell we find ourselves in was paved with the best of intentions. In Google's quest to get rid of traditional info gatekeepers and bring useful information to the masses, the learned skill of critical thinking has taken a staggering hit. It was too much too fast and people aren't equipped with the critical thinking and/or Digital Discernment skills to process it all.

The egalitarian Internet Google strives for unwittingly ushered in "*The Death of Expertise*", which is a phenomenal book I recommend enthusiastically. The one-sentence summary of that book is the issue with the average Joe that hinders understanding is they mistakenly believe expert opinions and regular opinions are of the same weight and value because ultimately, they're both opinions. This is inaccurate – dangerously so.

That's like saying, "The Pope is a priest". While technically accurate, that borders on being a lie of omission. The Pope isn't simply some priest. He's a priest who also happens to be the Head of State for the independent religious nation of the Vatican, and leader of one billion Catholics globally. That's a dramatic example, but you get my point.

Just as The Pope's opinion carries more weight than Pastor Tony down the street, an expert opinion carries more weight because it's based on subject matter expertise. Meaning this person has done the work and has the stature and standing to be able to speak from a place of authority. Now this doesn't mean that they're beyond reproach and can't be challenged, but it does mean their expertise should be valued as such and not lumped in with the common rabble.

Regrettably, subject matter expertise has been devalued in the wake of instant experts that have cropped up by the droves in the democratized Information Age Google has ushered in. These baseless and often dangerous opinions are like Uncle Ben's five-minute rice; but instead of "just add hot water", it's just add a slick website and nice landing page video and **BOOM** – you're an expert! While not totally Google's fault, they did create the conditions that birthed both the un-College Movement and #FakeNews; just as the Nixon and Reagan administrations created the conditions for the crack epidemic that birthed gangster rap. We'll break down these issues separately over the course of this book but will focus mostly on the un-College Movement and what it means for your future.

Not the Same Ole' Internet

A few things the skip College and "Just Google It" school of thought tends to neglect but you really need to understand are:

- Web 2.0

- Unknown Unknowns

- The Paradox of Choice

We'll briefly cover each below.

Web 2.0

The way Google used to work back in the day, is that when you typed in your search query, Google would return the best result based on the formula in its algorithm. It wouldn't really consider external factors. The results were based purely on the query itself.

This led to the unfortunate practice of keyword stuffing, where bad actors crammed in as many keywords as possible to try to artificially influence their organic search engine ranking. This is what's known as a "black hat" tactic. Black hat, for those who may be unfamiliar with the term, is any sort of trick or tactic where you're basically gaming the system or put bluntly – you're cheating! The opposite of a Black Hat is a White Hat, where you play by the rules.

You're living very dangerously with Black Hat tactics because here's the thing, that stuff works… until it doesn't! Some big-name companies have received Google penalties and gotten their sites de-indexed, which means Google completely drops you from the Google ecosystem, which includes YouTube, Gmail and the Google Display Network (GDN). And since Google gets the Lion's share of search traffic, you essentially don't exist to those using Google to search for your product or service, which again – is most people. So you want to avoid being de-indexed like the plague.

The way Google works now with what's called Web 2.0, is that when you go to Google and type in your search query, Google is going to return the best result they have **and** combine it with the information that they have of you as an individual:

- What you watch on YouTube and other video services

- You're browsing history

- Who you're connected to in your social graph

- The types of things you buy online, etc.

They're going to combine all of that along with the search query and return a first page result that is unique to you. So my first page results won't be the exact same as your first page results, for the exact same search term, because our browsing behavior and who we're connected to in our social graph is different. And yes, there are legit privacy concerns. People understandably get all "Big Brother" on you, but there's actually a really good non-insidious reason that Google does this; and that is context.

As human beings our brains build context automatically. We naturally make connections about what we're talking about, when we're talking about it. However, that's a fairly tall order for a non-sentient machine. Don't believe me? I'll prove it to you. Let's do a quick word association. If I say the word "Chicago", am I talking about:

- The mid-western mega-city?

- The band?

- The Broadway musical?

- The movie based on the Broadway musical?

One word, exact same spelling and pronunciation, four very different meanings – all of which can be used by the same person depending on what they're looking for in that particular moment. In order for Google to be able to correctly figure that out, they need to know quite a bit about you so they can tailor their results to you.

So that's the first chink in the armor of the, "Just Google It" school of thought. It assumes that you're going to find the exact same thing as everybody else. That may or may not be the case depending on several factors. My number one result might be your number four result. And your number seven result may not make it on my first page at all!

Unknown Unknowns

There's this weird, often unspoken social phenomenon that comes with Google. Because there's so much information available, people feel that they should have perfect info at all times. A school of thought believes there's never an excuse to not know anything because you could have "Just Googled It". That's unfair and not a reasonable expectation to have of anyone, let alone yourself. I cringe every time I hear someone spout this nonsense.

The best way to think of Google is as an information Genie. It'll give you whatever you ask for, but you have to ask first! Your search results are limited to your search query – meaning you already have to know enough about what you're seeking to make the ask of Google. How then are you supposed to ask for something you aren't aware exists yet? The answer is you can't, because you don't know what you don't you!

Google will only help you with "known unknowns", to borrow from former Secretary of Defense Donald Rumsfeld. Google can't and won't help you with "unknown unknowns" because you have to ask first, and you still don't know enough to ask.

Your ability to ask questions is limited to your life experiences and what you've been exposed to. If you haven't experienced or been exposed to something yet, you can't articulate a search query because you have no concept of what you seek yet. The way we solve for this is through collaboration! By joining with others who have different life experiences, we broaden our own horizons, learn new things and discover new and different rabbit holes Google is all too happy to lead us down. But you have to make the ask first, which means you have to have been exposed and know what you're seeking first.

So be kind to yourself. I give you permission to take the immense, unreasonable pressure of being able to figure out anything off of your shoulders. That simply isn't a reasonable expectation to have. Now that's not, repeat **NOT** an excuse to be intellectually lazy! It is simply an acknowledgment that your ability to discover new things does in fact have limits, contrary to what the "Just Google It" school of thought would have you believe. You can in fact surface **most** things with Google's aid – most, but not all.

Analysis Paralysis

Another obvious yet overlooked issue with the "Just Google It" school of thought is called The Paradox of Choice. The Paradox of Choice basically says that the more options that you have, the more difficult it becomes to make a decision. Some simply sum it up as analysis paralysis.

Have you ever been paralyzed while doing research? You go to Google; you type in your search query and BOOM! Less than a second later you're hit with millions, if not billions of search results, and you can't make heads or tails out of any of them! Overwhelmed and afraid you'll make the wrong choice; you don't make any choice at all. Well friends, you're not alone. The Paradox of Choice is a harsh reality the "Just Google It" camp chooses to ignore.

One of the ways people overcome The Paradox of Choice when shopping online is by looking for clues and shortcuts in the form of ratings and reviews. The problem with this is that a lot of that stuff can be faked! Take me for example, I co-wrote a book along with a fellow Full Sail grad called *Beyond Buzzwords: Social Media, Mobile and Other Marketing Buzzwords Ain't the Half of It*. We are dying for reviews! I mean we are hurting badly for them (if you're reading this right now and you actually bought my first book please, please, please leave a review on Amazon). Now, if I was less than ethical and so inclined to, I could go to a website called fiverr.com and pay someone to review my book. I could even pay them to do a video review. I would simply mail them a book, they would hold it up as proof they bought it, then proceed to read whatever pre-written review I sent them. I could get my reviews that way, five bucks at a time. But the reviews would be as fake as the day is long – no thanks!

There's a really good book on the topic called *Manipurated* by Daniel Lemon. It goes into detail about the great lengths people go through to cheat the ratings and reviews system. But as an ethical professional I don't do such things. Let's be clear, I've been on this journey called Digital Marketing since 2003/2004; it took an additional year to write that book. So when you read *Beyond Buzzwords*, you're literally holding 12 years of my life in your hands. I genuinely want to know what you think! No fake reviews…

Additionally, being self-taught is an inherently reactive process; meaning, "I need to know how to do this – so I'll go off and I'll learn this" or "I need to be able to do that – so I'll go off and I'll learn that". Being self-taught tends to be heavy on short-term tactics and light on long-term strategy. You'll often find yourself hip-deep in something before you figure out that you need to pivot, with huge gaps in your knowledge.

And so those are just the base issues with the school of thought that says, "just Google it". It does not take into account Web 2.0, Unknown Unknowns or The Paradox of Choice. It assumes that people have the skill of Digital Discernment while most simply don't.

Chapter 2: Lived Experience vs Opinion & Theory

This chapter is going to be a retrospective of my experience getting a bachelor's degree in Digital Marketing from Full Sail University. I'm not one of those self-proclaimed Digital Marketing Ninja/Guru/Mavens. I didn't just wake up one day and decided to give it a go. I'm not a mommy blogger, no dis to the mommy bloggers and all the self-taught individuals out there. I think if you were able to strike off on your own and figure out how to make a living from Digital Marketing at a professional level **without** having to borrow $57,000 from the U.S. Department of Education; that's awesome and amazing! I admire you from afar and am openly envious of you.

But then you have the rest of us; The other 99.99% where that just flat hasn't been our experience. I'm unashamed to say I had to go to College before I really became skilled at Digital Marketing. In my experience from talking to other people and small business owners at conferences, most of them can't figure it out on their own either. So, hats off to you if you were cold enough to skip College. But that's not me or most people.

I'm talking to the majority of folks who might be considering going to College, or just need a different side of the equation. I don't feel that those of us with formal education have done a very good job of speaking up and speaking out when prominent people like your Gary Vaynerchuk come out and tell young people not to go to College. I think people need to hear a different point of view from someone who has actually gone through the process.

Just so that I'm clear, when it comes to structured education, I am biased – NOT bougie! I don't think that everybody needs a degree. I certainly don't think everyone has to follow the same path as I have (it wasn't much fun – I'll spare you the turmoil if you let me). But again, there's a lot of chatter in the space that simply isn't objective enough. Those of us with a different experience need to step up and add to the conversation.

So first things first, most people who are of the opinion that you should skip College and "Just Google It" fall into one of three buckets:

- They don't have a degree at all. So, they're just anti-structured education in general.

- They have a degree, but it has nothing to do with what they currently do. For example, in Digital Marketing you'll find that most have degrees in journalism or computer science, which is secondarily or tertiarily related to Digital Marketing – but it's not their core competency.

- They have a general marketing degree or an MBA. They took a class in social media or had Digital Marketing as an elective. But again, it's not their core competency.

I on the other hand, from front to back, beginning to end, my entire degree; my elected major is Digital Marketing. It's my core competency. I'm part of a very small, elite minority. As of this writing there are less than five thousand of us with this professional credential. It's growing and our ranks are swelling, but by no means is it commonplace as of yet.

Shortly after graduating Salutatorian from Full Sail University's Digital Marketing Bachelor of Science program I wrote a blog post that you can find on my LinkedIn profile called, "Five reasons your five reasons may suck". It was in response to a blog post I saw on the Surviving After College blog named, "Five reasons you may not need a degree in Internet Marketing". The reasons it listed for skipping College in this career path are as follow:

- The industry changes too fast.

- The jobs don't require a degree.

- Those years could have been spent gaining experience instead of studying.

- You're overpaying.

- You can easily create your own online business.

Again, let me reiterate that when it comes to structured education, I am biased – but I am not bougie. I'm not here to convince anyone they should or shouldn't go to College. I just want to give a different perspective based on facts and lived experiences instead of opinions and theories. You have a lot of these blog posts like the one I'm discussing here, some from prominent people in the industry spouting off about things that technically they're un-educated about because they've never been through the process. Whereas I on the other hand, I have.

If I were to grade this, I would give this a **Triple D**:

- Dangerous

- Dated

- Does more harm than good

Misconception 1: The industry changes too fast to be taught in College.

You're making several assumptions here, but we'll address two. Firstly, you're assuming that the instructors are teaching from the halls of academia and aren't actively involved in the industry. While I can't speak for all post-secondary institutions, in the case of Full Sail University that simply isn't the case. Most, if not all of the professors have their own Digital Marketing agencies where they actively service clients; or have been on either the brand or agency side (or both). They're not passively teaching about an industry in which they don't actively engage.

An awesome podcast that I listened to, that I recommend you listen to as well, is the Marketing Smarts podcast by Marketing Profs.

It's hosted by former Full Sail University Professor Kerry O'Shea Gorgone. One of her past guests was James Loomstein, an adjunct professor at the Southern Methodist University Cox School of Business. He's also the managing partner at Rogue Marketing. He's a perfect example of why you shouldn't assume that you're getting stale information just because it's coming from College. Without spoiling the joy of listening to that episode, suffice it to say the man is the genuine article.

Secondly, you're assuming the course curriculum is static and not dynamic. I started attending Full Sail University in October 2012 and graduated in March 2015. If you look at my transcripts and compare it to what's up on the curriculum now, it's a very different program. The core stuff is still there, of course:

- Paid search

- Mobile marketing

- Email marketing

- SEO

- SEM

- Funnel optimization

You know, all the good stuff you'd expect from a hard skills perspective. But there are also some new courses like The Psychology of Play that I've been meaning to audit, which explores gamification. That wasn't part of the program when I was coming through just a handful of years prior. So don't assume that just because you're being taught in a College setting means that the curriculum is set in stone, because it's not. It does in fact change to keep up with the rapid pace the industry. At least in the case of Full Sail University – again, I can only speak for the things that I've been through.

Misconception 2: Most jobs in the industry don't actually require a degree.

This isn't incorrect, but it is incomplete. I graduated from the degree program in March 2015. In May of that same year, I started a job at Cox Media Group in Atlanta as an SEM Manager. Cox Media Group is a media conglomerate, they own television stations and newspapers. The same small business owners that advertise on the evening news or in the newspaper i.e. lawyers, plumbers, doctors etc., we would take that ad spend and put it on Google Ads.

To get that job you had to be Google Ads certified. You actually had to have all of the Google Ads certifications, not just fundamentals and the advanced search, but also mobile, video, shopping. That job didn't require a degree. I was one of two employees on the search team who had a degree in Digital Marketing. All you needed were your certifications. However, that's quickly becoming not the case, especially if your goal is to work at a large corporation like Cox Media Group or Procter & Gamble (P&G) like I have.

Additionally, assuming that you don't need a degree ignores some very powerful megatrends that are acting upon the industry. For example, I used to watch this makeup show on the SciFi Channel called *Face Off*. It's a competition show where they do fantasy movie makeup that you would see on Star Trek, X-Men or something like that.

They give the Twitter handle of everybody on the show. During the commercial breaks they want you to tweet using the show hashtag (#) for a chance to win $10,000. Using Twitter to run a hashtag competition is fairly old hat as of this writing, but that was unheard of ten years ago. Nobody was doing that, not that they couldn't, brands simply didn't.

This is a sweepstakes strategy that combines both social media and mobile, because most people use Twitter on their mobile devices. So yes, it is correct that a lot of the time the folks in these positions don't have any formal training in Digital Marketing, but as the industry progresses, measurement improves and strategies get more elaborate, companies are looking for specialized skills above and beyond what being self-taught typically provides. Just because you may not need a degree now does not mean it'll be that way in the future. I can't speak for you, but my philosophy is I'd rather have it and not need it, than need it and not have it!

Let's be frank – back in the day when Digital Marketing, specifically social media, first started to take off most big businesses were just waiting for the whole thing to blow over. Leadership at large companies like P&G didn't take it seriously and thought "a degree in Facebook" was stupid. Yet here we are 10-15 years later; the digital economy has matured and boasts some of the largest companies in the world.

The open secret that some mature folks still won't cop to, is that back in the day if you were just a little bit tech savvy, you got deemed the "tech person". Not because of education or training, but you were capable of opening your email or working the copying machine without blowing it up at a time when most couldn't. Then, all of the other "tech stuff" that came down the pike fell in their lap as the de-facto expert (or at least someone who could figure things out). But again, going forward this is not the case and de-facto expertise won't be enough in a mature Digital economy.

Misconception 3: You could have used that time gaining experience in the field instead of going to school.

So… remember what I talked about in the first half of this chapter about people just flat not having the skill of Digital Discernment? Not all experience is good or even applicable. While Google is doing its level best to crack down on the spread of #FakeNews and misinformation, there's still a lot of bad info out there and you might find yourself taken advantage of and not even know it.

Going back to the *Manipurated* book example, believe it or not, the people offering to post fake book reviews for you on fiverr.com don't think they're doing anything wrong (even though they're clearly cheating). You let them tell the story, they're just providing a service in the gig economy, no different than an Uber or

Lyft driver. Regrettably, they got sold a bag of goods by a bad guru they didn't recognize as such. If your Digital Discernment skills aren't up to parr you can find yourself on Warrior Forum or some other seedy part of the web getting information that you don't recognize as black hat or cheating. That can get you in a lot of trouble.

Quick story: I was four, maybe five months into the degree program and I had to take an English class. The English teacher asked us to list the top people in our field. The first name out of my mouth was Frank Kern! Up until that point, I thought he was THE Digital Marketer of all Digital Marketers. I listed out:

- Frank Kern

- Ryan Deiss

- Yanik Silver

- Eben Pagan

A lot of the folks that you'd find on Warrior Forum back in the day. She gently had to let me down and shared with me an article from TheVerge.com that had a scathing YouTube video attached to it, basically pulling back the curtain and exposing that whole racket.

Even after that, I wasn't convinced. I was like, no! That was biased – Frank Kern is awesome!! These people don't know what they're talking about. They're jealous of his success. They're a bunch of haters. Frank Kern is the dude.

Finally, she was like, dude, look at the industry level digital marketers and conferences we're exposing you to, you are never going to see Frank Kern on one of those stages. You're not going to see Frank Kern at Salesforce Dreamforce, or MozCon or something like that. He's just not going to be there. Do you really think that's because the conference organizers don't know about him? No – it's because he can't survive the vetting process and they don't want him on their stage.

Mind blown as my hero-worship of Frank Kern was forcibly ripped from me, it was then that I finally began to appreciate that there were levels to Digital Marketing. You have your corporate/industry level digital marketers; then you have your salt-of-the-earth info-marketers. There are levels to the industry that prior to I really didn't appreciate, because all I knew was Warrior Forum and info-marketing products. As a result, I picked up a lot of bad habits I didn't even realize I had, just like the poor folks selling reviews on Fiverr.com.

So degree programs like the ones offered at Full Sail University are going to keep you out of trouble and steer you away from some of the sketchier parts of the Internet. Again, when I was learning this stuff and self-taught, I didn't actively recognize it as Black Hat or whatever. I just thought I was learning the game from somebody who knew the game. Does that make sense?

Now my list looks completely different. This is just a taste of the pure awesome that graces my Twitter feed, but now I would say:

- N. Liberty White (@i_am_liberty)

- Jason Falls (@JasonFalls)

- Kerry O'Shea Gorgone (@KerryGorgone)

- Jay Baer (@jaybaer)

- David Meerman Scott (@dmscott)

- Tara Reed (@TaraReed_)

- Wil Reynolds (@wilreynolds)

- Mike King (@iPullRank)

- Joe Pulizzi (@JoePulizzi)

- Ann Handley (@annhandley)

The list goes on and on; but again, a totally different atmosphere and strata of the industry. If you're "Just Googling It" and are self-taught, you're not necessarily going to appreciate those subtle nuances. Not that you can't, of course, but it'll be more difficult.

Misconception 4:
You're overpaying.

I once heard a parent say, "I'm not paying to send you to College for something you can learn on YouTube for free". On the surface that seems fair enough, but let's unpack that. We've already covered Digital Discernment, so let's have a quick conversation about the different types of capital and access to capital, shall we?

There are only two things you can invest: time and money. We'll start with the later first. When it comes to monetary investment, YES – there's a lot of great FREE information out there in bits and pieces. But contrary to what the "Just Google It" crowd would have you believe, the time investment to aggregate it all from the four corners of the Internet is not insignificant. If you're someone who values their time and has the financial wherewithal to do so, simply paying to have someone else (like a College or University) do all the vetting for you is often a better use of both time and money.

Yet and still, there are high quality paid online courses that are a fraction of getting a bachelor's degree. However, you have to have the money up front! These range anywhere from a dollar (literally one dollar) all the up to several thousand dollars. I'll spare you the history lesson on those of us in the African diaspora, but needless to say the wealth gap is a thing and Black folk tend to be on the wrong side of it. Asking those of a lower station in life to drop several hundred to several thousand dollars on an online course just ain't happening in many cases.

But by far the most common way people professionalize themselves, network and disseminate best in class practices is via conferences and seminars. Prior to the global pandemic of COVID-19 which forced many of these events online – thereby lowering the cost, they were held in-person at hotel ballrooms or convention centers and were VERY cost prohibitive!

Take Funnel Hacking Live by Russell Brunson and the good folks over at Click Funnels. Funnel hacking is basically where you reverse-engineer online sales funnels. In the DMBS program at Full Sail University we just call that your final project. **Spoiler alert!** It's not exactly an apples-to-apples comparison, because at Full Sail your capstone is a team project. So there's that whole dynamic where you have the team captain who's responsible for making sure everything gets done, blah, blah, blah. But if you know how to funnel hack as defined by Click Funnels, that's more or less your final project in Full Sail's Digital Marketing bachelors' program.

As of this writing (mid-2020) Funnel Hacking Live general admission tickets were $997. They also had youth tickets available for $797, but you had to buy an adult ticket in order to purchase a youth ticket. That does NOT include your:

- Flight

- Car rental or Uber/Lyft

- Hotel or AirBNB

- Eating out for however many days

- Parking and other incidentals

Nope… just to have your face in that place is a cool thousand dollars. Once you add all that other stuff back in, you're probably looking at about $3-$5k per person depending on where in the world you're traveling from.

But that's not even an expensive conference. IBM Think, which is IBM's flagship conference on business & technology and THE conference to attend in the data community, is $2,700. Their 2019 conference was in San Francisco which is one of the most expensive cities in the United States. Depending on where you're traveling from, that could easily set you back $8k-$10k per person, total investment.

A lot of times these live events you'll have the opportunity to join a VIP coaching program, which in my experience ranges anywhere from about $10k all the way up to $50k depending on the industry. Just to keep the numbers round, let's say you drop $3k on Funnel Hacking Live and another $12k on their VIP coaching program. That's $15k to learn Digital Marketing from Click Funnels.

Yes, in aggregate $15k is a lot less than $57k for a degree from Full Sail University, but you've got the money up front – out of pocket! Russell Brunson is not going to accept financial aid. I'm sure he would if he could, but that's not how it's set up.

The open secret in the industry is that most everyone is there on the company's dime. Almost no one pays to attend these conferences out of pocket. Which means you already have to be working in the field to make it to one of these things. It's a vicious chicken/egg, catch 22 cycle that can be incredibly difficult to penetrate from the outside as someone still cutting their teeth in the industry.

As a result, if you look at the composition of these things in terms of the audiences, they tend to be Lily-white. And by that, I mean 85%-95% of the audience is going to be White because that's who,

- Are working in the roles at companies that can afford to send you

- Has the disposable income to afford the out of pocket expense (a tiny minority of attendees)

These are the unpleasant realities the "Just Google It" crowd conveniently leaves out. John Lee Dumas of Entrepreneur On Fire talks about his journey getting to where he is today. He found a lady to mentor him by the name of Jamie Tardy. He was paying this woman

$2,000 a month – out of pocket! There'd have been absolutely no way I could have swung that! And no, not because I'm not willing to invest in myself. You don't borrow $57,000 from the U.S. Department of Education by being unwilling to invest in yourself. No – it's not because I'm not coachable. I actually finished my degree program, including being broken of bad habits I wasn't aware I had! This means I'm both teachable and I'm coachable. There's a lot of people who went to College and didn't graduate. Whereas I on the other hand, I took everything my instructor said in and I executed. All those attributes aside, given my socio-economic station in life, there was just no way that I could have swung that high out of pocket threshold.

Coaches price their services high like that on purpose to keep the riff raff out. The problem is that that riffraff disproportionately tends to be Black people like me. It's like how fishermen go dragnet fishing for tuna and accidentally snap up a sea turtle. They didn't set out to catch the sea turtle, it just got caught in the net, but regardless they're still having turtle soup for dinner.

So yeah, if you're looking to acquire a professional skill set that doesn't require a professional license to practice **and** you got a spare $15k-$20k; you'll probably make out better with a private VIP coaching from [insert

Guru's name here] in your industry. However, if you don't have that type of disposable income lying around, the fact that $15k is less than $57k is of no utility to you because you can't access the $15k.

This needs to be addressed. It has to be talked about because the first step in solving a problem is admitting that there is one. You have these expensive conferences, these very expensive training programs, and then the even more expensive degree program. And there's not a lot of middle ground.

Misconception 5: You can easily create your own online business

Don't confuse simple for easy; those are two different things. While it's undeniably as simple as it's ever been to create an online business, entrepreneurship in any form isn't easy. It's "easy" in the same way losing weight is "easy"; eat less – exercise more. But as anyone who has ever struggled to lose weight will tell you, easy is the last adjective in the world to describe that process. Again, it's simple but not easy.

Furthermore, being a business owner isn't right for everyone and there's no shame in having other aspirations. Entrepreneurship in general, but digital entrepreneurship in particular, gets overly glamorized and even fetishized – kind of like marriage. Yes, it can be a beautiful thing, but you can also crash and burn! Don't believe me? Just ask somebody who's been divorced or had a failed business.

I'm not one of these entrepreneur hype-bros who love the game for loving the game's sake. I was seeking to solve an issue in my life (name discrimination) that took the form of digital entrepreneurship. If the solution took another form I would have just as readily accepted that. I didn't necessarily want to be my own boss. If I found a legit opportunity where I got paid fairly for my expertise and I still got to travel and speak professionally, I wouldn't turn my nose up at it.

Take somebody like Tom Webster, who's a VP for Edison Research or Brian Solis, Global Innovation Evangelist at Salesforce Marketing Cloud. These two gentlemen are respected thought leaders, top of their craft and also employees! So yes, it's simple (not easy) to create your own online business, but entrepreneurship is not right for everybody and we shouldn't force it down people's throats. Just as it is wrong to blindly expect everyone to go to College – it is equally wrong to pressure everyone into entrepreneurship. Context is key.

So there you have it, point by point rebuttals for some of the common reasons why people think College is of no value. As someone who's actually been through the process, I hope this shed some light and gifts you a different perspective.

Chapter 3: Unearthing Everyday A.I.

It's Already Here

Let's do another quick word association. If I say, "A.I." What images come to mind? Is it Will Smith fighting for his life in a dystopian Sci-Fi action thriller? Or Allen Iverson if you're a basketball fan? Maybe it's Shia LeBeouf matching wits with a rogue military A.I. bent on killing The President of the United States in *Eagle Eye*? But if action isn't your thing, maybe you'd even consider falling in love with one like Joaquin Phoenix in the movie *Her*?

What if I told you the truth was far less dramatic? What if I told you A.I. quietly entered our lives in the form of the lowly Email? That's right – Email! It's not as sexy and doesn't get the headlines like its scandalous cousin Social Media; but make no mistake, Email is the undisputed heavyweight champ of the Digital Marketing world and where most of the rubber-meets-road A.I. happens in real life. Checking

Email is the number one activity performed on a mobile device, not social media. That's why Facebook split off Messenger into its own stand-alone app, to get a piece of that Email pie.

But why are you telling me about how Email is actually A.I. in a book designed to debunk the un-College movement? Fair question. But to be clear, this book isn't about the un-College movement or #FakeNews and misinformation so much as it's about your agency in decision making. And that has **EVERYTHING** to do with A.I. and the types of messaging you get exposed to. Just stick with me.

Artificial Intelligence (A.I.) is where all industries, but Digital Marketing in particular (the change makers per Seth Godin) are beginning to go. A.I. is an increasing part of the puzzle; in some ways that are obvious, but most are far more subtle (some would even say insidious – but I'll leave the melodrama for the tinfoil hat crowd).

I'm a big, BIG fan of the Social Pros podcast by Jay Baer and the good folks over at

Convince and Convert. Way back on episode 266, guest LaSandra Brill (@LaSandraBrill) talked about how Artificial Intelligence is where Social Media was 10 years ago. This is a really profound, deep statement because if you think about the time frame she's referencing, MySpace was the Big Dogg in social media. Facebook was a small fry, if you can imagine that, and only for college students still. Fast forward to the landscape that we have today and many young people have never heard of MySpace! It's still out there, but it's changed form several times. Facebook and its suite of companies are the bona fide Big Doggs in the Social Media space, worth hundreds of $Billions of dollars. It's an entirely different landscape.

This has ushered in an era to where there's so much content being created it has far outpaced a human being's capacity to keep up, let alone make sense of it all. According to Statista, as of May 2019 there were 500 hours of video uploaded to YouTube every minute. That equates to approximately 30,000 hours of newly uploaded video content per hour. And hold onto your hat – 82.2 years' worth of video per day! For context the average life expectancy in the U.S. is 85 years. It would literally take nearly your entire life to watch a day's worth of new uploaded videos as of 2020.

That's just one content format on one platform. After you add back in the other video platforms like Netflix, as well as text messages, pictures, infographics, podcasts and emails; you're literally talking about hundreds of years' worth of digital content being created every single minute! There's simply no way we mere mortals can keep up with this insane pace. Even the Flash would struggle to keep up, and he's the Flash!

Artificial Intelligence (A.I.) is how we actually deliver on the promise of marketing, which is the right message to the right person at the right time. Consumer's expectations are getting higher as well. People expect you to remember their information with as little as one encounter. The days where you call into your bank or your airline, and they have to transfer you to five or six different departments, all of whom ask you for the same information over and over again are quickly going the way of the dinosaur thanks to A.I. But as with everything in life, there are tradeoffs. It is essential we don't lose our agency in the deal.

From Camels to Cars

In addition to Jay Baer, one of my professional man-crushes is Avinash Kaushik, or just Avinash for those of us who know and love him. Avinash writes a blog called Ockham's razor. As he's prone to do, he wrote a masterpiece of a blog post called "*The Artificial Intelligence Opportunity: A Camel to Cars Moment*". If you know Avinash you know his articles tend to be on the long side, but they're very, very informative – totally worth the time investment.

He starts by defining some terms to clear up any confusion. As with any new and burgeoning space, people tend to conflate terms that aren't necessarily the same. A.I. or artificial intelligence is an intelligent machine. Machine learning is the ability for the machine to learn without being explicitly programmed. Then there's deep learning, which is a specific machine learning technique.

Those terms get lumped together and thrown around a lot, but they are actually different things. It's important you understand the distinction between them. What excites Avinash the most, and is very exciting for me as well, is a machine learning, the ability for the machine to learn without being explicitly programmed.

Marketers like to toss around the word "revolution" a lot; mobile revolution this… digital revolution that ect. Oftentimes the reality doesn't quite live up to the hype. A.I. is no exception. It has actually been around since the 50's, believe it or not. They built this machine the size of a room that could play checkers. And for a long time, the promise of A.I. hasn't lived up to the hype. There was this term called the A.I. tundra because there were no real results to back up the hype. However, this is quickly becoming not the case as outlined in Avinash's blog post. A.I is finally coming up with the good as we experience yet another technological leap just as when we went from traveling on camels (and other 4-legged animals) to cars.

Trapped in Bubbles of Our Own Making

In my opinion, the un-College movement is based on a series of egalitarian myths of this idealized future state there's simply no evidence of. We really need to pay attention to the role A.I. is playing in popularizing this mindset; more specifically machine learning because it already affects us in our everyday lives. Let's go deeper into unpacking and debunking the "Just Google It" myth.

That is the foundation of the un-College movement is based on the premise that you can find information via search engines without having to pay for it. But most people don't understand how Google actually works, as well as how Google and Facebook keep us in what's called content bubbles. That is, they show us things that they think we'll like based on prior behavior so that we'll stay on their platform longer.

The reason they do this is because both Google and Facebook are advertiser supported. They need us to stay on their sites for a long period of time so we can engage with advertising. Whenever something is free, that's because you are the product. Google is free. Facebook is free. Guess what that means? Bingo! Advertisers pay them for the right to access the very large audiences they were able to garner with their free product.

Google and Facebook use machine learning to figure out your likes and your wants. In the case of Google, they personalize your search results based on a number of signals,

- who you're connected to in your social graph
- your browsing behavior
- what you watch on YouTube
- what you've recently purchased, etc.

The big takeaway here with regards to machine learning and how Google and Facebook tailors their results specifically to you, is that they use a boat load of signals to come up with what they're going to show you. At any given time, there can be upwards of 1,000 notifications waiting on you when you log into Facebook. But clearly Facebook doesn't show you all 1,000 in chronological order – that would be ridiculous. It uses its machine learning algorithm to surface what it thinks will be of the most interest to you.

There's also a fair chance you may be running a different version of Facebook than everyone else. In a rare interview on the Masters of Scale podcast with LinkedIn founder

Reid Hoffman, Mark Zuckerberg explains why he runs 10,000 versions of Facebook a day. Here's a short excerpt:

"At any given point in time, there isn't just one version of Facebook running, there are probably 10,000. Any engineer at the company can basically decide that they want to test something. There are some rules on sensitive things, but in general, an engineer can test something, and they can launch a version of Facebook not to the whole community, but maybe to 10,000 people or 50,000 people— whatever is necessary to get a good test of an experience," he shares in the podcast. "And then, they get a readout of how that affected all of the different metrics, and things that we care about. How were people connecting? How were people sharing? Do people have more friends in this version? Of course, business metrics, like how does this cost the efficiency of running the service, how much revenue are we making?"

A.I. is the Data Analyst

It's getting it to the point where machine learning may do away with the role of the analyst as we traditionally know it. The algorithm can decide to run the tests Mark Zuckerberg mentioned above on its own without any prompting. Because A.I. can crunch a lot of different signals very quickly that it would take a long time for us as human beings to come up with, they can predict the value of a customer to the company, which is a signal where they use past behavior, then they look at current behavior expressing the intent. Then based on that, they look at the predictive value to the company and they put that all in the context that the human being is in; all of this happens within a fraction of a second. It's really crazy.

So the point that Avinash makes in his article is that as analysts, we answered known-knowns. In a previous chapter I referenced,

- Known-Knowns: Things that you know you know
- Known-Unknowns: Things that you know you don't know
- Unknown-Unknowns: Things that you don't know that you don't know

Take me for example, I know that I know how to drive a car. I know that I know how to produce a podcast. This goes into the first bucket of known-knowns.

Then you have a second bucket of things that I know that I don't know. I know that I don't know how to fly a plane, because I'm not a pilot. I know that I don't know how to deliver a baby, because I'm not an OBGYN. These are all known-unknowns.

Finally, you have a third bucket, which are things that you don't know that you don't know. These are things that I don't even have a concept of. It's not that the information doesn't exist or that it's inaccessible, it's that I don't even know enough to ask Google the question! You literally don't know where to begin – that falls into the third bucket of unknown-unknowns.

Per Avinash's masterful insights (you really should take the time to read – it's listed in the references), the role of the analyst is going to shift away from talking about known-knowns, things that we know that we know, to solving for unknown-unknowns. Marinate on that for a minute. Really let it soak in... we'll soon have the ability to answer questions that we don't even know need to be answered yet! That will be the role of artificial intelligence, because machine learning is going to get so efficient at solving for the known-knowns, that Data Analysts in our current form now will no longer be necessary.

Greater Works Shall You Do

This is actually really exciting because personally, I'm not a Luddite. I'm not afraid of the future. I think the future is bright for those who embrace it. Only time will tell if I'm naïve and my faith in the future is misplaced, but I'm all for letting the machines handle things that we do by rote and repetition, thereby opening us up to do things that only human beings can do, which is being creative. At least, creativity is the providence of man at this point in time.

Avinash talks about the difference between intelligence and consciousness. Intelligence is the ability to solve problems. Consciousness is the ability to feel things. As we all know, our machines are intelligent. That's why we call it a smartphone. The device can solve problems and can figure things out, but it's not conscious (yet). But one of the most exciting things about A.I. and machine learning that really has Avinash turned on, me as well, is what he calls complete day one knowledge.

"When an elder dies, it's like a library burning to the ground." ~ African proverb

There's an old African proverb that when an elder dies, it's like a library burning to the ground. 70, 80, 90, or more years of wisdom simply gone that's never coming back, but with A.I. complete day, one knowledge that is no longer the case.

The analogy that Avinash uses is if you take a medical doctor like a dermatologist, within the span of their entire career (30-40 yrs.) they will look at around 200,000 cases. Obviously, the more practice you get and exposure you have in any discipline, the better you are at it. The problem is that there's really no way to transfer ALL the knowledge of those 200,000 cases on to a brand-new dermatologist just starting out. Sure, you have an apprenticeship program. You can mentor, train and tutor new dermatologists, but that entire body of knowledge over those 200,000 cases over the span of that 30-40 year career more or less gets lost when that dermatologist retires and no longer sees patients.

With A.I. that's no longer the case. One of the many miracles of artificial intelligence and machine learning is all of that accumulated knowledge is stored and future A.I. can access it. So when there's a new iteration of dermatology A.I., sticking with the example, they have the benefit of having the knowledge of all 200,000 cases of its predecessor and nothing gets lost during transfer. That really doesn't exist in the context of human beings. Some information is going to get lost with the passing of the torch from one generation to the next, but with A.I. nothing gets lost.

It's a brave new world. This literally changes everything. And there's already numerous examples of how artificial intelligence is better at diagnosing medical issues in humans. You have several cases where you have actual doctors looking at forms of skin cancer, melanoma, and the artificial intelligence is as good or if not a little bit better at predicting and diagnosing those results. It's really, really exciting stuff.

This Singularity Cometh

Again, I'm doing my best to keep this book within the realm of Digital Marketing as change makers in an effort to preserve agency in decision making, but there is this thing called the singularity. This is when futurist predict that A.I. will become as intelligent and as sentient as a human being. And the date keeps creeping up! At first, guys like futurist Michio Kaku were saying that the singularity will happen in 2045. Now I've heard reports of 2035, and even as early as 2029!

Irrespective of when the singularity actually shows up, the fact is that it's well on its way. It will happen within our lifetimes. I don't know about you guys reading this, but I'll still be alive 30 years from now. I'll be in my sixties, but I'll still be here.

So as marketers, educators and those generally concerned with agency we really need to get on the ball and get ahead of these things because there are ethical concerns that come into play about people being manipulated. Going back to the #FakeNews example, people were manipulated during the 2016 election. There's no denying it.

Pizzagate

Some poor man got ahold of this cockamamie scheme about Hillary Clinton orchestrating the abuse of children out of a Pizza Factory. This self-appointed hero decides he'll not brook this outrage, grabs his gun, goes to his nearest Pizza Factory and starts firing off shots. I kid you not – that happened in real life. Someone could have died because of a #FakeNews story.

Without getting into the whole politics about who should have won in 2016 blah, blah, blah, because that's a done deal; people were manipulated, and they got taken advantage of. That brings in ethical concerns about what Cambridge Analytica did. On the one hand you can argue that Cambridge Analytica did their jobs and they did it well. On the other hand, you take exception to the notion of their tactics being described as a good job.

Bringing it back to the role A.I. play in what we're exposed to and preserving agency in decision making, I for one am not fearful of the implications. I'm not afraid of losing my job. I don't think there will ever come a time where human beings will not be needed in some capacity. I might be naive on that, and I'll be the first one to admit it. Who knows? But personally, I am really looking forward to a future where A.I. becomes an even more dominant player in the Digital Marketing space.

I'm already using A.I. in my business. Having run search, social media and email marketing campaigns for some of the largest companies in the world – me and A.I. are buddies. Yes, there are privacy and ethical concerns. Yes – it's scary! But regardless AI is here and it's here to stay. Let's continue down this path of preserving agency in decision making together.

Chapter 4: Digital Discernment is a Life Skill

"T. Adeola is the number one resource to teach you the reality of the digital media & marketing landscape to propel your career. He's an activist who advocates for high professional standards in the education and execution of digital media and marketing."

That was the impact statement I came away with after winning a one-hour consulting session with my fellow podcaster, author and advertising industry "Mad Man" Park Howell from The Business of Story. The clarity and confidence he instilled in me after our one-hour session on his podcast is precisely the feeling I want to give you after reading this book.

It takes a lot of skill to be able to pull that off in as little as an hour, because most people's brand story is fuzzy and ambiguous. They have an idea what it is, but it can be very elusive and hard to put your hand on. Park is a master of pulling your brand story out of you and refining it in a way that not only makes sense, but that you can actually monetize (turn into money)!

During this process, Park asks what your why is. Why are you doing this? Why do you do what you do? It turns out that I'm actually a career counselor. My why – the deep-seated reason that I do this after you peel back all the layers, is that I'm an activist who advocates for high professional standards in both the education and execution digital media and marketing.

One of my former guests on *The Marketing Disenchanted Podcast*, Jay Akunzo, had a pinned tweet on his Twitter profile that sums it up nicely, "The downside of the Information Age is advice overload". I'll be more candid and just call a spade, a spade. There are a lot of false prophets and fake gurus online. They wreak havoc on people's businesses and careers by giving poor advice and instilling bad habits their victims don't even know that they have! This is abhorrent and repugnant to me. I'm dedicated to putting a stop to it as a former victim.

You're Not Dumb – You Were Duped!

True story: Back when I lived in Dayton, OH before relocating down to Atlanta, GA I was involved in my local Real Estate Investors Association, GDREIA. I know… I know, it sounds like a venereal disease, but it's not! It stands for the Greater Dayton Real Estate Investors Association. All of the REIA's, which is an acronym, R.E.I.A. which stands for Real Estate Investors Association, they all have a reciprocal relationship with one another.

Every now and then you'll have a speaker who has hit GDREIA, Cincinnati REIA, Columbus REIA etc. as they tour the State of Ohio. Vena Jones Cox, who is one of the premier Real Estate wholesaling teachers in the country is based out of Cincinnati, OH. She brought in a speaker out of Baltimore, MD who is a Digital Marketing expert, but also a REIA leader out there. He was speaking about how he uses digital marketing to rent and sell his properties and all the success he's had. He also takes on clients for which he promises to produce the same results. Vena invited the speaker to Cincinnati REIA, but he made a stop at GDREIA while he was in the area.

How these things usually work is that, whenever there's a speaker in town, they'll come speak to the general membership for free. Then typically that weekend or a week later, they'll have a paid closed-door training session. The cost is low enough to be accessible, but still significant enough that you're invested and people actually show up; somewhere between $97 - $150 depending on who it is.

I liked the guy, nice brother out of Baltimore, so I paid the $97 bucks or whatever for his weekend training in Columbus, OH. Vena Jones Cox also runs the Columbus, OH REIA in addition to being a major figure in the Cincinnati, OH REIA.

I get there and there's probably 50 people in the room. The speaker is going over all of the tactics and strategy that he uses to market his properties online. I kid you not, this brother got up there in this room, a paid room folks – everybody in this room paid $100 to be there; this man tells these people he still keyword stuffs! My jaw literally dropped at such a brazen admission. I'm like, "What did you just say?"

I'm not the type to make a scene in public, so I don't make a big kerfuffle about it. But after he was finished speaking, I approached him gently and ease into saying, "You know keyword stuffing isn't a best practice, right?" He replies, "Yeah it's not, but it still works so I still do it."

This was back in 2013, shortly after I had first entered Full Sail University's Digital Marketing degree program. When I talked to this brother, who's a good guy — by the way, I'm not trying to paint him with a dirty brush; I very much so got the sense that while he knew what he was doing at a base level, he didn't fully appreciate the implications and long-term ramifications of some of the tactics that he was engaging in and espousing to others.

It's kind of like how everyone knows overeating and eating foods high in salt is unhealthy and leads to obesity — which leads to a host of other health issues. It's one thing to know that, it's quite another to change your behavior; especially if you're a broke College student and Ramen Noodles and canned sardines are the only things keeping you alive (though they're dreadfully high in sodium and are a fast way to develop high blood pressure). That's very much the vibe I got from this "guru" out of Baltimore. He was aware what he was doing wasn't the best, but like a broke College student doing they're level best not to starve he didn't fully appreciate just what was at stake and how dearly that could cost him in the long run.

Had to Shut Him Down

The guru out of Baltimore also submitted a proposal to GDREIA to do some digital marketing for them. I was also the chairperson for the newly formed Wholesale subgroup at the time. As such I got to go to the board meetings, though I wasn't actually on the board and didn't get to vote. But I did get to weigh in on topics and speak my peace, even though I was a nonvoting member.

The proposal this guy presented was actually very thorough and went through specifically how he would be getting web traffic for GDREIA. Tucked off in the appendix this dude had a link farm! For those uninitiated in SEO, link farms are old school black hat tactics that are no-Bueno. It's the equivalent of a mountain of cheeseburgers from The Heart Attack Grill (yes – that's an actual restaurant).

I still have a copy of that dubious proposal; which I will not publish in this book, I don't want to get sued. I've been very careful about not mentioning the guy's name. But yeah, he submitted a proposal to our real estate investors association, and he had a link farm and a bunch of other black hat SEO garbage in it. I love to see my brothers winning, but I was duty bound to shoot his proposal down. Again, I didn't get to vote since I wasn't an elected board member. But I strongly recommended GDREIA take a pass on his services, which they did.

More Than Just Money – Standards!

Again, the point of that real-life example wasn't to paint the brother from Baltimore with a dirty brush, but rather to shine a light on the damage that's caused when unsuspecting students learn bad habits from bad teachers. But since the students are as green as a blade of grass, they're defenseless against these charlatans. For the record, the GDREIA board was gung-ho about this guy's proposal until I put a stop to it. They had never seen a link farm before and didn't know it was black hat SEO, so they didn't know it wasn't above board. But they did know enough to ask me and thankfully, and trusted me enough to follow my recommendation not to proceed.

So you have these unsuspecting practitioners like the brother from Baltimore that get ahold off bad teachers that they don't recognize as such because cheating makes money. Since the student is using money as the success metric, the teacher comes off smelling like a rose. The naïve thinking goes, "Well I'm making money at it. That means it's working because if it didn't work, I wouldn't be making money."

If only life were that simple! There's a lot of unscrupulous things you can do that make money but aren't the best for your reputation. You can make a lot off of selling drugs, guns, your body and/or the bodies of others. All those things make money if you lack standards and basic moral compass. But black hat SEO is more difficult to spot than drug dealing, gun running or prostitution.

You're running a very big risk engaging in black hat tactics, especially if you're taking on clients! If you get a client a Google penalty and their site gets de-index, you're getting sued! They're going to look to you to recoup the money they lost when their site was down. Quiet as it's kept, big companies like JC Penny's, Overstock.com and BMW have all received Google penalties messing around with black hat consultants they didn't know were black hat. They just thought, "Oh, they're gurus. They make money at it so they know how it works". Then messed around and got de-indexed!

So the stakes are really high when you're talking about whom you get your information from. In the context of COVID-19 some people actually died because of bad information. Not to be overly dramatic, but the skill of Digital Discernment is literally a matter of life and death at this point!

That's why I do what I do. That's why I'm compelled to podcast, write books and speak. Because the brother from Baltimore is not unique in so far as he was blithely repeating garbage. You have a lot of folks out here like, "Hey, I'm a guru. This works." But just as drug dealing "works" in so far as it produces revenue, they haven't thought through that they're damaging or risking their professional relationship. If you let him tell the story I'm sure he would reply with some version of he was just learning the game from somebody who knew the game – which is how getting turned out always starts, with misplaced trust.

He went to Warrior Forum or wherever and got a course and started doing what he was taught to do. Even though he engages in black hat tactics, he doesn't actually view himself in those terms. From his perspective this is just how the game is played. As I've said before, I did not learn the term black hat until I came to Full Sail University. I used to be in the same boat.

Here's more inside baseball for you, black hats don't call each other black hats! That's a term the industry itself put on them for their unscrupulous behavior, but they don't actually call themselves that or market themselves that way. They call each other Ninjas or Gurus or even Mavens. So again, when you're as green as a blade of grass – which we all were at some point, you can find yourself in the clutches of these cheaters and not even know it!

Revisiting the *Manipurated* example from Chapter One, because it bears repeating, I could go to fiverr.com and pay somebody to give my book a five star review. There's an entire cottage industry and courses on Warrior Forum dedicated to gaming the system (black hat). If you don't have a level of knowledge and sophistication to know what's black hat and what's not, you could be forgiven for thinking, "Okay, I'm learning the game from somebody who knows the game." Because that's how these cheaters present themselves. It's not going to register to you that you're actually cheating and engaging in things that aren't above board. You're still new and don't know what you don't know.

The thing about being a black hat and why I come down so hard on it is because there's no such thing as being a little black hat. Kind of like how there's no such thing as being a little pregnant. You're either pregnant or you're not. When you come to black hat tactics, you either cheat or you don't – simple as that. I know we're all out here chasing money, but we got to have some principles!

Principles Over Profit

Going back to my man Jay Akunzo's Twitter profile, on June 13th, 2017, Martin Lieberman tweeted that "There's hardly any traffic when you take the high road." That's what this guy actually tweeted. True to his nature, I love my man Jay Akunzo, Jay tweeted in response,

"The right thing is always the right thing. Make a great show and the marketing gets easier. Avoid the gimmicks. Do right by your audience, period."

Be that as it may, the unpleasant reality is that it's deeper than that because before you can do right, you need to know what's right and what's wrong! Building that context is getting harder and harder. If Warrior Forum is all that you know and have been exposed to; you're not going to be aware that your beloved guru is actually a black hat because at this stage in your journey you don't have anything to compare and contrast against.

Not a Monolith

Again, the definition of success online needs to be broader than just making money. Digital Marketing is not a monolith. Like a lot of people, when I first came to Full Sail University, I equivocate Digital Marketing with Social Media.

If we did a quick word association (because you know how much I love those) and you said to me "Digital Marketing", my knee jerk reaction would have been "social media". But the digital media and marketing economy is vastly larger than that! I used to compare it to the medical field and that is very broad and there are several areas of specialization, but I think a better way of explaining it is to say that,

"Saying Digital Marketing is Social Media is like saying Walmart sells toys."

And for the record Walmart does sell toys. They're the number one toy retailer, especially around Christmas time. Walmart is so very good at selling toys they killed-off one of the retail highlights of my childhood, Toys-R-Us. But they also sell:

- Groceries
- Jewelry
- Guns
- Gaming consoles
- Electronics
- Televisions
- Clothes
- Prescription medication
- Pet supplies
- Auto repair

The list goes on for eternity, but if you're a Walmart shopper you get my point. There's a lot of things Walmart sells above and beyond toys, even though again, they're the #1 retailer of toys and put Toys-R-Us out of business.

It's the same with Digital Marketing. Yes, Social Media is a part of Digital Marketing. But just like Walmart sells more than toys, Digital Marketing is much, MUCH bigger than just Social Media. That's something not enough people have gotten their heads around.

Just like there's a lot of different things that you can buy at Walmart; There are several different career paths in the digital economy that have little or nothing to do with Social Media. You can get into

- Email marketing
- Cyber security
- Project management
- Data analytics
- Data ethics
- Technical writing

There are several different or ways that you can go about professionalizing yourself. It's really going to come down to your circumstances, what you want to do, the space in the digital marketing ecosystem that you want to occupy.

F.A.A.N.G. – Bigger than You Think

If companies were countries and market cap were gross domestic product or GDP; the F.A.A.N.G companies:

Facebook

Apple

Amazon

-N- (and)

Google

Combined they would be the 3rd largest Country in the world behind the United States and China. They're four of the five most valuable companies in America (the 5th is the above-mentioned Walmart) and account for ¼ of the United States GDP.

Individually, if companies were countries and market cap were gross domestic product or GDP:

Apple 10th largest > GDP of Canada

Amazon 13th largest > GDP of South Korea

Google 19th largest > GDP of Turkey

Facebook 22nd largest > GDP of oil rich Saudi Arabia

So when we say "Big Tech" it's really, REALLY big!! So big in fact that you can't pigeonhole it to just social media or even coding. I hope this example helped bring that home. With that new context I hope this short chapter helps you realize the various layers to the digital economy and why HOW you are introduced to it is so very important. Things are different now. A bad guru could cost you dearly, which is why at this stage of the game, Digital Discernment is a Life Skill.

Chapter 5: The 3 A's

In chapter one I gave you blow-by-blow rebuttals to five common misconceptions of the value of getting a degree in Digital Marketing. This chapter we'll go broader than just Digital Marketing, as well as be benefit focused instead of going on defense. That's right, in this chapter I'll give you the actual benefits of post-secondary education in the Information Age of #FakeNews and Misinformation.

Spoiler Alert: it is not, repeat **NOT** access to information or learning how to do something. As we all know by this point, you can do that on YouTube University for free – which is the root misconception of the un-College Movement.

In entrepreneurial circles I often hear degrees referred to as, "a piece of paper" (much to my chagrin) – as though all pieces of paper are equal or some nonsense like that. It's not just any piece of paper – it's a receipt of the highest order. A receipt that certifies you have met high standards and are of sufficient quality.

But proof aside, there are many non-tangibles that are just as, if not more important than the hard skills and training you receive in College. I call them the 3 A's:

- Access (to capital)
- Alumni Association (social capital)
- Acumen (professionalism)

It Takes Dough to Make Bread

Student loan debt is a HUGE issue – there's no denying it. While I'm not here to trivialize that, the flip side to that coin is it's also the sole means of access many of us have. I've already talked about the high cost of conferences and seminars pre-COVID19, so I won't belabor the issue here, but without the access provided Federal Student loans, I for one simply wouldn't have been able to access the professional level information I needed out of pocket.

Another quick example of why access matters so much, and why I HATE the deceptive false narrative around not needing it in the entrepreneurial community, can be found in the book *THE ONE THING* by Gary Keller with Jay Papasan. In the book the authors talk about how you need at least One Person willing to take an active role in your success. For Sam Walton of Wal-Mart fame, early on that person was his father-in-law, L.S. Robson.

Sam's daddy-in-law loaned him $20k for his first retail business, a Ben Franklin franchise store. But when Sam was ready to open his first Wal-Mart store, his kindly poppa-in-law secretly paid the landlord $20k for a pivotal expansion lease.

For context, L.S. Robson did this for Sam Walton back in the 1950's. Adjusted for inflation, that same $20,000 in 1950's dollars are worth a whopping $216,000 as of this writing in the year 2020. Sam Walton's father-in-law did this for him not once, but TWICE!!

The reason this aggravates me so is because it's in stark contrast to the Conservative/Libertarian ideals of self-reliance and pulling yourself up by your bootstraps on your own strength (even and especially if you don't have any boots). However, if you do even a little bit of digging, you'll quickly discover that behind every "self-made" ultra-wealthy person there's a rich daddy/uncle lurking in the background. This self-made false narrative is rampant in the entrepreneurship community but simply isn't factual. No one makes it alone – NO ONE!

Back in the 1950's Black people were doing well not to get lynched, let alone build wealth. Due to systemic racism, specifically as it pertains to acquiring wealth via real estate as outlined in the book *The Color of Law* by Richard Rothstein; the Black community simply doesn't have the resources and familial wealth to invest in our children the way L.S. Robson invested in his son-in-law Sam Walton. Therefore, that investment has to come from someplace else, and in the case of College, yes – that means student loans. But just as Sam Walton felt no shame in accepting help from his father-in-law, let no one shame you into feeling bad about taking out a student loan. I for one thank God for that level of access and don't begrudge it, because without it I'd still be on the outside looking in.

It's Not What You Know – It's Who You Know

Money is but one form of capital, believe it or not there are actually nine. By far one of the most valuable, some would argue even more than money, is social capital!

Fun Fact: As of this writing <u>ALL</u> of the U.S. Supreme Court Justices, literally all of them without exception, went to either Harvard or Yale University. Coincidence? I think not.

The point I'm making with this example is that certain Colleges and Universities have in-roads, even foot holds, in certain industries. Take my alma mater, Full Sail University, for example. Here's an excerpt from my first book, *Beyond Buzzwords: Social Media, Mobile and Other Marketing Buzzwords Ain't the Half of It!*;

"For those who don't know, Full Sail University is a well-respected digital media school. Its graduates run the gamut in the entertainment industry from one mixing Pharrell Williams' platinum song Happy, to another working on popular video games franchises such as Call of Duty, Halo and Grand Theft Auto; as well as many movie blockbusters including The Avengers, X-Men and The Hunger Games. From The Emmys to American Idol, Grey's Anatomy, Scandal, How to Get Away with Murder, professional sporting events in the NBA, NFL, MLB and everywhere in between;

there isn't too much of the entertainment business a Full Sail grad doesn't touch in some capacity.

And then you have us lowly Digital Marketers, by far the black sheep of Full Sail University. We may work in the entertainment industry or we might work at a bank. Who knows? Just about everyone needs Digital Marketing services nowadays so we aren't limited to one industry. At best we're about five percent of the student body. Really, it's probably closer to around three percent, but it's my story and I tell it how I want; so I say the number's five-percent."

Just as with Harvard and Yale in the Supreme Court example, if you're looking to get into the entertainment business Full Sail University has one of the best alumni associations you could possibly ask for. Alumni regularly come back and speak with current students and the professional networking within the industry is second to none. The social capital that come from being able to say, "I graduated from Full Sail University" is worth its weight in gold in the entertainment business.

So contrary to popular belief, College isn't just about obtaining a "piece of paper" (though receipts are vastly important) or learning how to complete a task. You're joining a family when you become an alumnus of a distinguished institution of higher learning. And family looks out for each other.

People Skills (or lack there of)

I'm a member of the much-maligned Millennial generation. One of the main critiques my generation receives from older generations like Baby Boomers is that we don't know how to talk to people. Or in other words, we lack professional acumen.

You'll hear Gen-X and Baby Boomers say disparaging thing about Millennials, like:

- No boundaries
- No respect for our elders
- No filter – will say the first thing that comes to our minds
- No commitment – will quit a job in a heartbeat

Clearly, I don't agree with all of these criticisms, but I'll concede that they're not entirely baseless. Acumen is one of the tougher non-tangibles to come by. There's no hack, no quick & dirty way to come by it. While there are certainly approaches you can take that work better than others, really you just have to jump in and deal with other people.

College forces you to be around people who are different than you. You're going to have to learn how to deal with the loud roommate or that butt-hole Professor that you can't stand, but ultimately, they control your grade for this semester. From a social development standpoint there's no substitute for these life experiences, as you will encounter these same people and personalities in the workforce.

The unpleasant reality is that the only way to develop sagacity and get good at dealing with difficult people, is by dealing with difficult people! College forces you to develop that skill if you hadn't already.

The subject of English has always come very easily to me. Math, not so much, but I have never struggled with the English language. So imagine my shock and appall when I received a D in English-I at Sinclair Community College! My teacher's name was Elizabeth Christiansen and we couldn't stand each other. I can't even remember why we hated each other so much, but we did.

She graded my papers as though they we doctoral dissertations. I didn't have an inch! My papers would come back bloody red from all the marks it received, though I was clearly one of the strongest writers in the class. Classmates who were weaker writers than me would get B's but I got a D?

I went so far as to appeal to the Dean, but she told me with kind resignation that because Elizabeth Christiansen was tenured, there was nothing that could be done. Even if I appealed directly to the President of the College, the only way my unjust grade would be changed was if she changed it.

Needless to say, I felt as though I got a raw deal, but there was nothing to be done about it. I then went on to ace English-II with an A+. My English-II teacher even remarked how shocked she was that I got a D in the previous class, since I'm such a strong writer and communicator.

But this type of scenario isn't confined to the classroom. It happens in the business world all the time. You run afoul of a higher up, and they have the capacity to either ruin your career or drive you out of the organization (or both). I'm not saying it's right or fair, but it is reality. This was a hard lesson for me to learn, but I'm glad I learned it. Because this unpleasant experience was in a classroom setting, it didn't come at the cost of my career. Sucked though it did, a D is still done! I was still able to continue matriculating towards my Associates Degree.

So, there you have it! The actual benefits of going to College in the Information Age where YouTube University is free. The 3 A's:

- Access (to capital)
- Alumni Association (social capital)
- Acumen (professionalism)

To be clear, I'm not asserting College is the only means by which to acquire these non-tangible benefits. But again, there are only two things you can invest – time and money. You can learn anything without formal education, but it will typically take you much longer and you'll make more mistakes than necessary. Investing in education is often a wiser use of both.

Chapter 6: Time & Trajectory

Time is the one commodity you can't get back

The point of view of this book, as well as most everything I create is; I am talking to myself 10 or 20 years ago. Yes, I know it's an overused cliché, but "*if I knew then what I know now*" what would I have told my younger self? That of course assumes I would have listened to my older self, which honestly, I probably wouldn't have.

Confession: in terms of career trajectory – I wasted my twenties! I spent the better part of that decade "just Googling it" trying to figure things out on my own. It took fatherhood and the introspection that came with having my first child before I was ready to make a professional investment in myself. The harsh reality is that time could have been better spent, had I but known how to spend it.

Yes, I know, from the philosophical point of view time is never wasted. Each decision leads you to where you need to be at any given point in your journey. Change the decisions and you change the journey, which means you wouldn't be you, but some other version of you i.e., somebody else. There's no telling if that other version of you would be happier or even better, simply other. So, no matter where you are at this point in life, be grateful for your journey and that you've been given another day. As the saying goes,

"Yesterday is history. Tomorrow is a mystery. But today is a gift, that's why it's called the present."

I get all that – but this ain't a philosophy book nor am I speaking philosophically! As it pertains to my career trajectory as a professional Digital Marketer, there's no denying my 20's were in fact underutilized.

If you look at some top Digital Marketers as of this writing, many are my contemporaries.

Take industry leaders like:

- Wil Reynolds, @wilreynolds
- Mike King, @iPullRank
- Brian Fanzo, @iSocialFanz
- Carlos Gill, @carlosgil83

We're roughly the same age, give or take a few years. However, they made certain choices in their twenties that set them up for the professional careers they have now that I didn't make. For example, Mike King and Wil Reynolds not only know how to code, but knew how to code back in the early 2000's. Back before coding programs were so ubiquitous and you really had to know what you were doing. They were able to take their coding abilities and parlay that into technical SEO, which they then parlayed into professional speaking and stood up their own Digital Marketing agencies; iPullRank and SEER Interactive respectively.

I didn't take the time to learn how to code back in the early 2000's. If you knew me back in 2002, you'd know what a huge miracle it was for me to graduate High School on time! After graduation I was too busy blithely chasing a quick buck on Google, not because my character was flawed, but because I simply didn't know any better at 18 yrs old. Nor did I have anyone in my life with the industry foresight and influence to set me on the right path. I was directionless and had no concept of just how valuable the skillset of coding would be just 10 – 20 short years later. It allowed the above-mentioned men to set themselves up for success in a manner that's hard to overcome at this stage of the game now that coding has become more mainstream and ubiquitous. My prayer is this book plays that role for you and I can save you some heartache and regret.

Navigating Professional Trauma

I hosted and produced a podcast in 2017 called The Marketing Disenchanted Podcast. I consistently released an episode a week, every week that entire year. The last question that I ask is a modified version of the last question that John Lee Dumas asks on his Entrepreneur On Fire podcast (Yes fellow members of Fire Nation, I did ask permission). I changed it as follows:

"Imagine you woke up in a brand-new world, identical to earth but you knew no one! You still have all the experiences, knowledge and skills. Your food and shelter are taken care of, but all you have is a laptop and no money. That's right! You are college freshmen broke, baby. You've got somewhere to lay your head, a meal plan, Internet WiFi, and that's it. How would you build relationships with industry thought leaders over the next 30 days by working for free?"

Why did I ask that question? Why did I structure it the way I did? Well, there's the stated reason that I give in the interviews, which I'll cover here in a little bit, but then there's the real reason that I ask that question. Prepare for an instructive tale of woe about an unfortunate experience with this person I met via networking.

She was the head of CEO Space in Atlanta. CEO Space is for lack of a better term, a behind the scenes incubator for products, services and professional development in general – though it doesn't meet the technical definition of an incubator in the Start Up/ Venture Capital space, which is a different animal entirely. A lot of top personal development speakers like Les Brown or Lisa Nichols, they went through CEO Space. The product Airborne, those effervescent tablets that you drop in water to boost your immune system, that came through CEO Space as well. The promise and main benefit are connections that can take your career to the next level. Think ABC's Shark Tank, but not as mean or formal.

Through her involvement with CEO Space, this woman picks up her own personal clients. One of them who shall remain nameless, she charges $15,000+ for strategy. However, she doesn't know how to fulfill it on the back end. So, the CEO Space lady was trying to get myself and our company, Digital Marketing Advisers, to do the fulfillment for her client.

On the fulfillment side of Digital Marketing, it's easy to get taken advantage of. Fulfillment has been commoditized to a large extent. Thanks to sites like fiverr.com you can get folks in the Philippines or India for a fraction of what someone like myself State-side would charge. You've got to be careful when dealing with people who may only want to pay offshore prices for premium work, which is essentially what happened.

In addition to getting beat up on price, this person had an unfortunate experience with a prior service provider, which is not uncommon. I'm a long-time listener of the Social Pros podcast by Jay Baer. In the first episode of 2016 he had on people from The Agency Management Institute to talk about their 2015 hiring and firing report. The podcast episode was on why agencies get fired so often.

They surveyed companies with budgets between a half million and $4 million. A full **36%** of respondents said that the people who sold them these digital marketing services, they didn't get what they paid for. The unfortunate reality is that in the professional Digital Marketing space, a lot of people were faking the funk for a long time. So you have people out here who have been jaded and they really require a lot of nurturing upfront before they're willing to do business with you.

However, the flip side to that coin is that on our side as an agency owner and service provider, we have hard costs associated with running campaigns. It's not simply our labor. We use a number of pro tools like Reach Rocket by Marty Weintraub from Aim Clear out of Minneapolis. These pro level tools, in addition to our years of experience and know how, enable us to produce superior results. And those tools cost money!

Free-mium Fallout

So, we were at an impasse where this woman wanted us to build out the entire campaign upfront, do all this work in her account so she could review it; then and only then would she pay us. We're like look, that's not how we do things! In addition to our hard costs which need to be covered; in that scenario there's nothing stopping her from turning on the campaigns and revoking our access, then not paying us since they were already built out and running in her ad account.

Due to her previous trauma with bad actors in the space, she just wasn't willing to play ball fairly from our perspective. I confess, emotion got the better of us and that conversation wasn't handled appropriately. We were like, "How dare you"! Unfortunately (or fortunately) we did lose that deal.

I wouldn't go as far as to say the bridge had been burned with the lady at CEO Space, but that professional relationship did suffer. Since you never know which connection will be needed in the future, you want to avoid burning bridges as much as possible, though there will undoubtedly come times for necessary endings as outlined in this story. Still, handle them as amicably and professionally as possible.

So that's the real reason I asked the last question the way I asked it. For better or worse there is an expectation of receiving free work as popularized by books like *Rich Dad/Poor Dad* – and just Internet culture in general. There is an expectation of not paying for things online that you would otherwise pay for in the real world. Knowing how to work for free while still keeping the lights on and food on the table is something that you're going to have to figure out. It's a skill that you need in the Digital Economy.

Why Professionalism?

There's a huge gap in the professional Digital Marketing education space in terms of career trajectory. By professional I'm referring to someone who works in-house at a corporation or brand or works at an agency. I'm not referring to digital entrepreneurship or solopreneurs; somebody like a John Lee Dumas (JLD) or Pat Flynn. Yes, you can absolutely make the case that they're pros because they operate at such a high level, that isn't who I'm talking about.

I'm talking about people with jobs, as that's how most adults support themselves. Using my own experience and journey as an analog, what ends up happening is that folks meander the wilds of Google for a year or ten. They have some wins, they have some losses, pick up a few things and along the way get introduced to Warrior Forum, network marketing etc., that sort of thing.

At some point they acknowledge the time they've wasted, vow to never do it again and decide to get serious. Now they have three options:

1. Get a degree or certificate in Digital Marketing
2. Just Google it
3. Hit the conference/seminar circuit

We've already given quite a bit of ink to these options in this book, so I won't belabor the points here. But what I will say is that it's been my experience that professionalism is the gift that keeps on giving. Getting a degree and/or certificate is the only one of the three options listed above where developing acumen is baked in. With the other two you may, or you may not.

Be Gentle with Yourself

You're asking for frustration with options two and three above if you're from a lower socio-economic class like I was. I used to beat myself up a lot with negative self-talk like, "Why don't you want it bad enough? Why can't you figure it out? This person just hopped online and made it. If they can – you can. So what the heck is wrong with you?". When the reality is there's far more to the story than that, as discussed in previous chapters.

In marketing we use personas. They're fictional avatars with real characteristics that represent our customers. My avatar's name is

Lamar. He's 24 years old going on 25. He did not go to college after graduating high school at age 18. Unfortunately, he drank the Kool-Aid and "Just Googled it". But the whole un-College movement isn't really working out for him.

He spent the next six years after High School graduation having a series of wins and losses, but mostly losses. He tried his hand at network marketing and various rackets on Warrior Forum. So here he is 24 about to turn 25 years old. He has a two-year-old daughter that he's struggling support. And he stays up at night berating himself because he cannot provide the level of life that he feels his daughter deserves, or that he knows he's capable of.

He's at that age where had he just gone to College at 18, he would have graduated by now. Many of his friends have master's degrees and incomes commensurate with their education level. Having the benefit of six years of hindsight and a daughter he doesn't want to disappoint; he's at that stage where he's ready to make the investment. He's ready to go pro. However, he cannot afford going to conferences and has been around the block enough times to be wary of free lead magnets.

So that's Lamar; that's my avatar - that's who I do it for. I know that place, I know where that desperation comes from. As I've said before, I'll spare you some heartache if you let me.

Perspective is Everything

Again, online there is this culture that believes things should be free, which can put you in a bind because the high-quality content/services that people want for free actually cost money for you to produce. Going back to my CEO Space horror story, the women involved were older and I just kind of chalked that up to an old mindset. While I love me some Rich Dad/Poor Dad, let's be frank – Robert Kiyosaki is an old man and he thinks like an old guy. So I just thought that mentality and expectation was from a bygone era before we had officially entered the age of pay-to-play in social media.

Imagine my shock while listening to the Social Pros podcast by Jay Baer of Convince and Convert, he had on Nick Cicero, the original co-host of the podcast. Jay has since had Jeffrey K. Rohrs and now Adam Brown from Salesforce as his co-host. Nick Cicero stated he was surprised that not more people offer to work for free for him. To my astonishment Jay Baer readily co-signed that sentiment!

It caught me off guard because like I said, I thought this way of thinking was old and before we had officially entered the age of pay-to-play in social media; a phenomenon that was been discussed extensively on the Social Pros podcast and given quite a bit of ink on the Convince and Convert blog by Jay Baer himself. So to hear him of all people co-signed this sentiment made my jaw drop!

I sent Nick Cicero and Jay Bear the same email, which neither of them responded to. In hindsight the wording may have come across as harsher than intended. And because knowing what not to do is often times just as, if not more instructive than knowing what to do, I'll post my ill-fated email below:

Email Title: Pay-to-play – but Still Work for Free?

Salutations Jay! (Because salutation is more fun than hello.)

I really enjoyed your recent interview for Social Pros where you interviewed former hosts Nick Cicero. I was struck by a comment he made towards the end of the interview, where he stated he was surprised more people don't offer to work for him for free; a sentiment you readily co-signed.

I'm curious how you think that works in the age of pay-to-play digital media and in particular social media. Seriously, I'm just asking. That's not meant to be accusatory or anything other than genuinely inquisitive. You see, I've wrestled with this for many moons now, ever since first reading Rich Dad/Poor Dad over a decade ago. On the one hand, I absolutely see the wisdom in working for free as articulated by Robert Kiyosaki and others. But on the other hand, as you yourself has given quite a bit of ink to, the social media free ride is over!

We've officially entered the age of pay-to-play in social media, and digital marketing as a whole. So how is it that you expect someone to work for free in a pay-to-play space? I don't get how that works.

Here's where things really snap in my head. Let's say I'm willing to work for free, however, labor isn't my only cost of doing business. Whenever we run Facebook campaigns, we use a tool called Reach Rocket by Marty Weintraub from Aim Clear, who you should totally have on the social pros podcast, by the way (hint, hint, wink, wink). Sure. It has a free option, but the functionality of the free option is limited compared to what you need to provide professional services.

So even though I'm willing to put the time in at no cost, I still have a cost of doing business (Reach Rocket) which must be paid. And of course, Reach Rocket is in addition to the actual ad spend and other hard costs associated that must be paid for the campaign to run. Am I making sense here, Jay?

Again, I'm genuinely trying to gain an understanding of how this free philosophy works in your head, so I can make it work in mine. Because it just doesn't at the moment, not given the current climate of where Digital Marketing is.

I'm a huge fan and hope that you take the time to respond. I've been an avid listener of your podcast for years now, and really enjoy your work.

Kind regards,

T.

And as I previously stated Jay did not respond. Nor did Nick Cicero. But while I did not have access to them, I do have access to Kerry O'shea Gorgone, host of the Marketing Smarts podcast by Marketing Profs. That's actually how I became aware of Jay Baer in the first place.

Kerry was a Full Sail professor. I started listening to the podcast and through her I got turned on to basically everybody else. I listen to like 10 podcasts now, not exaggerating. And most all originated from either Kerry directly or the Social Pros podcast. She put me on to Jay Baer, Dorie Clark, Mark Schaefer, Mac Collier – everybody! It all has its roots with Kerry.

I reached out to Kerry whining like, "Kerry! Jay thinks I'm a hater. He won't talk to me. He hates me. It's the end of the world". Kerry, being the nice lady that she is, replies that while she can't speak for Jay, she's almost positive he wasn't talking about MarTech (marketing technology); the actual cost of the tools to use.

She then referred me to the MarketingProfs forum area where you can ask questions. I got a really good response that could have saved me a lot of turmoil with the CEO Space debacle I shared earlier, had I had it in my arsenal at the time. Here's the little script you can use when working for free that won't put you in a bad position.

"I'm eager to show you what I can do and how valuable I can be to your business. In fact, I'm prepared to work for free for the first month or two, because I know you'll want more once you see the value I can provide. All I ask is that you cover out of pocket expenses and commit to a media budget of at least $500 a month, billed directly to you by Google and/or Facebook. Out of pocket expenses won't exceed $100 per month, guaranteed. Sound fair? I know you won't regret this. I'm eager to show you what I can do for your business."

So there you have it! That little script could have saved me from learning the CEO Space lesson the hard way. If you plan to go the agency route and take on clients, I encourage you to make it your own and avoid any unnecessary headaches. Happy hunting!

Conclusion: One-Degree Over Chicago

In late 2020 my best friend Alan's younger cousin Keith was murdered in Mableton, GA, a suburb of Atlanta next to Smyrna. He was in town to celebrate his older brother's birthday. Keith had a bit of money on him and was flashing it. He caught the attention of a young lady at Applebee's who unfortunately set him up. Keith was killed during the robbery.

I've known Alan since we were four years old. We became fast friends in pre-school at Dayton Catholic and were practically joined at the hip until I moved to Nigeria during my middle school years. Up to that point I was at his house almost every weekend or vice versa.

We were no longer joined at the hip once I returned from Nigeria in 1998. We went to different High Schools and began to run in different circles, but we remained close friends. I was the best man at his wedding. Our friendship has endured a lot over 30+ years and I can honestly say at this point he's my brother, not a friend.

At the funeral I saw many of his cousins, including the deceased Keith, for the first time in over 20 yrs. The last time I saw Keith, around 1996 he wasn't even ten years old, now he's dead in a pine box; it was a surreal experience.

As per usual there was a slideshow of pictures of the deceased playing on a continuous loop prior to the service starting. There was one in particular that hit me different. It was of Keith, flanked by his older sister and younger brother. I'm not certain, but if I had to hazard a guess, I'd say they were 2, 4, and 6 yrs old in that picture.

It struck me because I remember that picture. I'd passed it countless times in the hallway of Alan's house. Now I have three children of my own who don't look too dissimilar. As a father, the thought of having to bury one of them is unfathomable.

Keith didn't have the easiest of lives. He served various stints in prison and had just got out three months prior to his murder. As such, there were varying degrees of thuggish/hood at the funeral.

As people came up to remember Keith, they all remarked about his resiliency. How he had the ability to smile through anything. No matter what he was going through, he never lost his smile. Several people remarked about how Keith would call from jail and cheer them up. His loved ones called Keith the Juggernaut, because he could go through anything.

It's said that if you're flying from New York to California, a one-degree change in trajectory over Chicago is the difference between landing in San Francisco or San Diego, which are 500 miles apart; 506 miles apart to be exact. A common mistake that people make is thinking that people who get incarcerated are ne'er-do-wells that wouldn't have amounted to anything anyway, but that clearly wasn't the case with Keith. This was evident by not only what people said about him, but by the fact that he packed the place out during a pandemic, that's how loved he was.

Keith was highly intelligent, caring and could lead people. He could have easily been a Director at IBM, GE or wherever. The economy lost out on not only a great talent, but a beautiful soul thanks in no small part to my sworn enemy, the school-to-prison pipeline.

Why do I end the book this way? Not to bring you down, but to impress upon you the outsized impact seemingly small decisions can have over time. One-degree may not sound like much, but it translates into a big impact over the journey from New York to California. The same holds true for life.

I'm not saying that going to College could have saved Keith's life. But what I am saying is that in most cases (not all – but most), College is a one-degree type of decision that has an outsized impact on the trajectory of your life. Remember that before you blithely drink the un-College Kool Aid as espoused by Darth Vee and his ilk. My sincere hope is that I've given you the perspective to do so. But regardless of what path that you ultimately choose, know that I'm rooting for you.

Here's to you!

About the Author

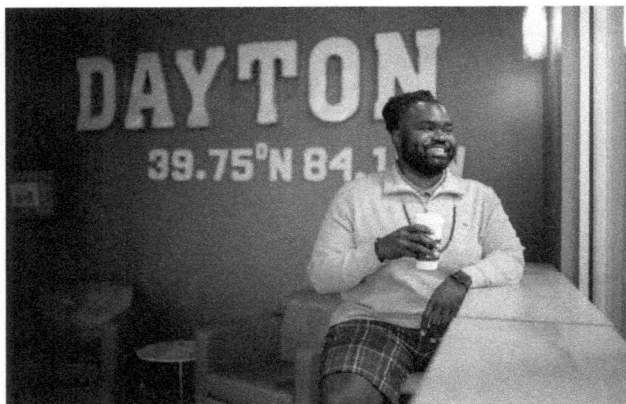

From the City that birthed flight, funk music, and the classic literature of Paul Laurence Dunbar; T. Adeola is the next classic hail from Dayton, OH.

A "pain in the teacher's class" turned successful Young Black Professional, T. Adeola transitioned from being a card-carrying member of "The Bad Kids Club" with chronic suspension, truancy and barely graduating High School to graduating Salutatorian from Full Sail

University's Digital Marketing Bachelor of Science degree program. From there, he went on to manage search, social media and email marketing campaigns for national and international conglomerates including Cox Media Group, ACCO Brands and Procter & Gamble (P&G).

Having managed interactive, digital and mobile programs of various complexities; now he's on a mission to pay it forward by helping troubled males of color escape the school-to-prison pipeline by tapping into their greatness and exposing them to the benefits of professionalism. To that end, he co-founded STEM Whisperers; a College & Career Readiness STEM Workforce Development Program designed to replace the school-to-prison pipeline with a Marketing Technology (MarTech) career path.

Learn more and get involved at stemwhisperers.com.

References

How Target Figured Out A Teen Girl Was
Pregnant Before Her Father Did

https://www.forbes.com/sites/kashmirhill/2012/0
2/16/how-target-figured-out-a-teen-girl-was-
pregnant-before-her-father-did/#2e9fbaad6668

This Analysis Shows How Viral Fake Election
News Stories Outperformed Real News On
Facebook

https://www.buzzfeednews.com/article/craigsilv
erman/viral-fake-election-news-outperformed-
real-news-on-facebook#.tjL9jYn2AZ

10 Big Brands That Were Penalized By Google,
From Rap Genius To The BBC

https://marketingland.com/10-big-brands-that-
were-penalized-by-google-69646

5 Reasons Your 5 Reasons May Suck!

https://www.linkedin.com/pulse/5-reasons-your-
may-suck-temitayo-a-osinubi/

Manipurated:

https://www.manipurated.com/

How to Own the Consideration Phase:
Professor James Loomstein on Marketing
Smarts [Podcast]

https://www.marketingprofs.com/podcasts/2016
/30723/buyers-journey-james-loomstein-
marketing-smarts

Scamworld: 'Get rich quick' mutates into an
unstoppable monster

https://youtu.be/Z0LZ6DNCgrY

Avinash Kaushik on Machine Learning
https://www.sixpixels.com/podcast/archives/spo
s_580_-
_avinash_kaushik_on_machine_learning_and_
artificial_intelligence_for_marketing/

Hours of video uploaded to YouTube every
minute as of May 2019

https://www.statista.com/statistics/259477/hour
s-of-video-uploaded-to-youtube-every-minute/

Why Mark Zuckerberg Runs 10,000 Facebook Versions a Day

https://www.entrepreneur.com/article/294242

Pizzagate: From rumor, to hashtag, to gunfire in D.C.

https://www.washingtonpost.com/local/pizzagate-from-rumor-to-hashtag-to-gunfire-in-dc/2016/12/06/4c7def50-bbd4-11e6-94ac-3d324840106c_story.html

Business of Story Podcast #102: Using the Story Cycle To Tell Your Story On Purpose

https://businessofstory.com/podcast/temitayo-osinubi-story-cycle/

Jay Acunzo Twitter

https://twitter.com/jayacunzo

25 giant companies that are bigger than entire countries

https://www.businessinsider.com/25-giant-companies-that-earn-more-than-entire-countries-2018-7

Global is the next avenue of growth for FAANG, and India is a core part of this growth

https://vested.co.in/blog/global-is-the-next-avenue-of-growth-for-faang-and-india-is-a-core-part-of-this-growth/

Agency Edge Research Series 2015

https://agencymanagementinstitute.com/agency-tools/agency-edge-research-series/research-2015/

Why Agencies Get Fired so Often

https://www.convinceandconvert.com/podcasts/episodes/why-agencies-get-fired-so-often/

www.ingramcontent.com/pod-product-compliance
Lightning Source LLC
LaVergne TN
LVHW011207080426
835508LV00007B/641